THE HOW TO STUDY BOOK

DR ALAN BROWN is a professor at Southern Methodist University in the United States. He is a memory expert and has spent more than 30 years researching the ways students learn.

Overcoming Common Problems Series

For a full list of titles please contact
Sheldon Press, Marylebone Road, London NW1 4DU

Overcoming Common Problems Series

Overcoming Common Problems Series

Overcoming Common Problems

The How to Study Book

Alan Brown

sheldon**PRESS**

First published in 2000 by Barricade Books Inc., New York.
This anglicized edition published in Great Britain in 2001 by
Sheldon Press, Holy Trinity Church, Marylebone Road, London NW1 4DU

British Library Cataloguing-in-Publication Data

A catalogue record for this book is available
from the British Library

ISBN 0–85969–851–3

Typeset by Deltatype Limited, Birkenhead, Merseyside
Printed in Great Britain by Biddles Ltd, www.biddles.co.uk

Contents

Introduction

When I began college teaching 25 years ago, I was struck by something odd. All of the students in my classes had been professional memorizers for 13 or 14 years, learning and recalling massive amounts of information. For nine months each year, their main job had been absorbing facts, then demonstrating the acquired knowledge through periodic evaluation. Even though this is the case, little attention is given to the student's basic survival skills – how to learn, study, and recall effectively. The students that do achieve success have done so because they have developed a personal strategy.

Suppose I employ you to perform a complex job – manage a small coffee shop. However, I give you no training on how to do it, but expect you to 'sink or swim'. Furthermore, I provide you with little feedback on how well you are conducting your business. Your only index of success is that you have not gone bankrupt. And to complicate things, I keep moving you from one shop to another and make your operation progressively more complex. This is similar to the situation that students face at school. The only true measure of success is whether you pass or fail tests. You are continually confronted with new teachers who have different expectations, and your academic job becomes progressively more complex as you advance through school.

Why are so few pupils taught how to study and learn effectively? Most teachers were never instructed in these basic learning skills. So they assume that their pupils don't need such training, either. In our culture, memorizing is viewed as necessary drudgery – a means to academic success. There is no glamour or excitement in memorizing. In fact, with the modern increase in the speed with which information can be stored and accessed, our mental methods seem antiquated by comparison.

The practical goal of this book is to provide strategies for studying more effectively and efficiently. Not everybody is cut out to be a straight-A student, but the techniques outlined here will make studying less arduous and stressful. It reveals successful students' methods of Attention, Encoding, Rehearsal and Retrieval, although other factors can influence your study effectiveness, such as motivation to succeed, relationship with your instructor, and time management. I will give you no hype or promises of an infallible memory. A number of books on the market promise a near-perfect memory or that you'll get nothing but A's once you read their book. Instead, the goal of this book is to provide the help you need to study more effectively as well as making studying less difficult. But first, some important questions.

Have you ever . . .?

- drifted off during class?
- been up all night before a test?
- crammed just before a test?
- become upset because a test is 'unfair'?
- failed to finish all the reading before a test?
- found your class notes confusing when looking back over them?
- got caught without enough time to finish a test?
- had to read the first page of your set reading two or three times?
- found your mind gone blank during a test?
- had difficulty finding a good place to study?

If you answered 'yes' to any of these questions, you will benefit from this book.

INTRODUCTION

Your time as a student is limited, so I promise to convey my points simply and directly. As a friend told me, 'The last thing a student wants to do is to study how to study. So keep it simple!' If you let it, this book will help you manage your memory, study more efficiently, and cope effectively with academic tests.

I should note that while some of the advice in this book is for college students – school teachers frown on people marking up textbooks, for example – much of what follows will help secondary school pupils survive and thrive through the rigours and tedium of irregular verbs, the periodic table and all the other things they need to know if they are to get good exam results.

Introduction summary:
Improving your study success

Principle One

The basic survival skills required for success are learning, studying, memorizing and recalling information accurately. The students who have achieved scholarly success have developed a strategy for learning what works in combination with their intellectual ability.

Principle Two

The strategies for basic survival skills are as follows:

- Attention
- Retrieval
- Encoding
- Rehearsal

These skills can be achieved with simple memory tricks.

Principle Three

Not everybody is a straight-A student. The strategies in this book are guaranteed to achieve more successful study. How far you take it is up to you.

How to read this book

Be selective

Don't read this book as you would a novel. You do not have to read it from beginning to end to find out what is going on. First, do a self-diagnosis to determine what you have the greatest difficulty with – taking notes in class, controlling test anxiety, completing the set reading? Next, read those chapters. Once you have addressed the most difficult areas, you can work on other problem areas one at a time.

Read backwards

As you tackle each chapter, read the summary at the end first to give you a clear picture of what will be covered. This gives your brain a road map to follow. Next, skim through the chapter for key words and phrases. Finally, read the sections that are of particular interest to you. Again, you do not have to read the entire chapter, beginning to end – rather, select the most important sections to read first.

Digest in small bites

In order to change your behaviour, you must tackle old habits bit by bit. If you wanted to improve your tennis serve, your coach would give you only a few things upon which to focus first, such as arching your back and keeping both toes on the serving line. After improving these, the coach would then give you a few more tips. Being a successful student involves complex behaviour patterns, so work on only a few aspects at a time. Attempting to change everything at once might overwhelm and discourage you.

Your strongest tool is your mind

Remember that the strongest tool that accompanies this guide is your own mind. You've chosen to take on the challenge and responsibility that goes with making the best of your education. This guide will provide the resources you need to help achieve those goals.

Good luck!

Alan S. Brown

Preview
The principles of learning

Before reshaping your study habits, a few principles of memory function might be helpful.

Information stages

Memorizing is like a mental assembly line – the raw material of new information is converted into memory packages through several steps. Information is first experienced by the senses (sights, sounds, smells) and then quickly passed into a mental-processing system called 'working memory'. Most data reaching our senses does not even make it to working memory. We select only a small part of the incoming information to pass along to it. After digesting this information for a minute or two, it is ready to be put in 'long-term memory' – on the library shelf of our mind. We can then make the information more accessible by repeatedly practising its retrieval – otherwise the path to the information may fade away.

Information

Sensory memory→ Working memory→ Long-term memory

Paying attention

The biggest struggle to improve studying involves attention, not memory. Have you been introduced to somebody and immediately 'forgotten' their name? This is not bad memory. It is bad attention. You did not forget the name. You never got it in the first place! The name never made it to working memory because you were distracted by your own thoughts – what the person looked like, how their voice sounded, whether they were going to like you.

A similar thing happens in class or when reading. Your attention wanders, and the information never gets into memory because you did not capture it to begin with. If you have great difficulty paying attention, you may want to refer to the material at the end of this chapter regarding special learning needs.

Creating associations

To get information to stick in long-term memory, it must be digested, customized or processed while it is in working memory. If you fail to personalize it in some unique way, it will be more difficult to remember. New information needs to be changed into a mental image, catalogued, reorganized or related in some way to information already stored in memory. It is like acquiring a new book for your mental library. If you don't label the book with a unique number, you will never be able to find it in your mental stacks when you go to look for it later. Processing new information through mental association makes it stand out in memory as well as making it easier to locate the next time you try to find it.

Revising

The final step in the learning assembly line is revision. Although a seemingly dry and boring activity, you are really practising recall. By strengthening your retrieval route to the information, a habit is being developed for accessing the material later. It's like finding a special spot in the woods and constructing a stone path to that place. Without occasional rehearsal, weeds may grow up over the path, making it difficult to make your way back to the spot

again. Looking at it another way, revision strengthens your
retrieval muscle.

Preview summary:
The principles of learning

Principle One: Paying attention

In order to remember, we must pay attention. This ensures that the information enters our memory-processing system in the first place.

Principle Two: Making the association

Once we capture the information, it needs to be customized or made distinctive. Otherwise, it cannot find a unique place in our memory store.

Principle Three: Revising

After we have stored the information, we need to practise finding it. Practising retrieval ensures that we establish a strong mental pathway to information.

1
Sensory modes:
How you learn

Your sensory modes strongly influence how you understand the world and relate to other people. We experience all information through three primary sensory channels – *kinaesthetic, visual* and *auditory*. Learning ability depends upon which mode(s) are most and least effective for each individual. Knowing your sensory-mode pattern will help you:

- appreciate the type of information that is easiest for you to remember
- understand why some learning situations are so difficult.

For example, suppose that you purchase a piece of furniture that requires assembly. You open the box and spread out all the pieces. What do you do next?

- Immediately start trying to put things together?
- Stop all activity and thoroughly read the instructions?
- Find a friend to talk to about the assembly process?

The first approach indicates a *kinaesthetic* learner. These individuals need an immediate, hands-on experience with something new. Kinaesthetic learners often achieve their goal through a series of forward and backward steps – put it together, take it apart, then assemble it again in a different way, and so on. Although it may seem counterproductive, these 'mistakes' are how a kinaesthetic person learns.

The second strategy typifies a *visual* learner's approach. These people can comfortably wade through a long series of instructions and mentally visualize each step in the process. In a sense, they assemble the furniture first in their head and then apply this to the real thing. The third approach is *auditory*. The auditory learner needs to hear what to do first by discussing it with somebody else or talking to themselves about the assembly process. Reading the instructions out loud may do at a pinch.

Read on to find out more about the learning mode that is most favourable to your method of thinking.

Kinaesthetic mode

The kinaesthetic person learns best from note taking, recopying notes and outlining the book. Most teachers have a visual/auditory strength and structure the classroom learning experience accordingly. Thus, both visual and auditory individuals are well served by the standard academic classroom experience, while kinaesthetic learners may be considerably challenged in this setting.

To keep the learning channels open, they require movement in some form. While note taking meets this requirement to some extent, their need for different varieties of motion is difficult to fulfil in a standard class period. Being allowed to stand up and walk around the room would help. Kinaesthetic individuals will often have several different places to study and move from one to the other while learning.

Visual mode

People with a strong visual mode learn best from books, handouts, writing on the blackboard, outlines, and class notes. Strong visualizers like to study by themselves rather than with others. They see the world in terms of categories and sort each new piece of information into an appropriate mental 'container'. Visual people do not integrate a complete learning experience until every new concept and piece of information can be put in a proper category, as if their mind is organized like a spreadsheet.

The visual person has a variety of mental categories for information, like the pigeonholes in the post room. Each new experience or fact must be placed in a particular box. If none exists, a new box is created. Visual individuals are usually very organized and require a neat and tidy environment to function best. They believe in paperwork and making lists. Loose ends bother them.

Auditory mode

Strong auditory learners prefer hearing the lecture, discussing material with others, and repeating the material aloud to themselves. The best indicator of an auditory individual is a tendency to talk to themselves. Information is not real until it is heard. Saying it to oneself may suffice. They have a very good memory of what was said and can often repeat the information verbatim.

Individuals with a strong auditory mode will often gravitate to study groups because the multiple auditory inputs help them solidify the material. Groups also give them an opportunity to speak, thereby strengthening their memory. Tape recordings of lectures are helpful to this type of individual. Some auditory learners outline their lecture and book material orally on audiotape.

Special learning needs

Attention deficit disorder

In recent years, there have been tremendous advances in understanding the effects of attentional problems on the learning process. Attention deficit disorder, or ADD, can cause serious impairment of a student's academic performance. The way in which this disorder has been defined has changed over the years. At first, it was believed that all these individuals were hyperactive (excessively active), but we now believe that only some attentionally impaired people have this dysfunction (attention deficit hyperactivity disorder, or ADHD).

Do the following quick quiz to see if you have signs of such an attentional problem. Do you:

- have problems completing tasks?
- find yourself frequently drifting off in the classroom?
- have difficulty sitting still?
- easily get frustrated with tedious or difficult tasks?
- have trouble with controlling impulse?
- feel overly distracted by unusual sounds or movement around you?
- find yourself jumping from task to task?
- note that teachers always seem to get upset with you 'for no reason'?
- have trouble completing tests in the time allowed?
- have quick mood changes or temper-control problems?

If four or more of the above characterize you, then you should be evaluated for attentional problems. Most colleges and universities have facilities to test their students. If not, they should have a referral list of community professionals who do such testing. Through a series of cognitive and intelligence tests, a specific pattern of results usually indicates an attentional problem. If testing reveals this problem, then you should see if special facilities can be offered. Adjustments involve mainly the elimination of time constraints in testing situations because individuals with ADD take longer to process information and their ability to 'stay on task' is impaired. Therefore, a time-limited test is unfair to them and shows them to be less intelligent or skilled than they really are. Another accommodation involves a separate testing room. Students with ADD may be overly distracted by noises and movement in the usual classroom, so taking examinations in a separate, distraction-free environment helps them perform better. Most college teachers are becoming sensitive to the issue of attentional problems and are willing to work with students to make modifications in the learning environment.

Language-processing difficulties

Another problem that can hamper academic success is that of language-processing difficulties. The way we decode and understand words and sentences is an extremely complex task. Some people's mental 'wiring' is not perfect. Problems may include a difficulty perceiving letters or sounds (known as decoding difficulties), making the mental connection between words and their meanings, or being able to express language in a written or oral form.

The way in which our brain processes cognitive information can have a major impact on our school performance. Most individuals with learning disabilities are unaware that they are different and don't understand why they are having so much trouble in school.

If you find reading, writing or understanding language to be very tedious or frustrating, you should consult the special needs teacher at your school. There are a number of ways to diagnose 'learning difficulties'. If you do have this problem, your school can do things to make your academic experience less difficult.

A test to help you determine your sensory mode

Now that you have been introduced to different methods of learning, you are ready to determine the manner in which you learn.

For the following statements, put a '1' beside the alternative most like you, a '3' beside the one least like you, and a '2' beside the intermediate choice. Then add up the scores under (a), (b) and (c). Compare your results with those of other people in your class to understand the many varied learning types among different students.

I would not like a job situation that:
(a)__ requires sitting at a desk all day
(b)__ is near a loud or repetitive noise
(c)__ is in an office without windows

I learn new techniques or procedures by:
(a)__ trial and error
(b)__ having it explained
(c)__ reading about it

After visiting someone, I remember best:
(a)__ what we did
(b)__ what we talked about
(c)__ how they looked

I can tell when people are nervous by the:
(a)__ way they move and hold their body
(b)__ sound of their voice
(c)— look on their face

I remember phone numbers by:
(a)__ pretending to touch the numbers
(b)__ saying them to check if they sound right
(c)__ seeing the numbers in my mind

To learn a new game, I:
(a)__ start playing and pick it up as I go
(b)__ have someone explain it to me
(c)__ read the instructions

16

I relax by:
- (a)__ going for a walk
- (b)__ listening to music
- (c)__ reading

When I have trouble finding something in a shop, I:
- (a)__ keep walking around until I find it
- (b)__ ask an employee
- (c)__ look at the aisle signs

I learn new techniques on a computer by:
- (a)__ trial and error
- (b)__ having it explained
- (c)__ reading about it

I am likely to get drowsy during a one-hour:
- (a)__ boring car ride
- (b)__ tedious speech
- (c)__ dull video presentation

When revising for a test, I:
- (a)__ walk around while reviewing the material
- (b)__ repeat key concepts aloud
- (c)__ visualize my outline

When doing a class project, I like to work:
- (a)__ with a friend
- (b)__ in a group
- (c)__ by myself

I learn new information well if:
- (a)__ a working model is provided
- (b)__ someone explains the concepts
- (c)__ graphs and charts are provided

When encountering someone I haven't seen in years, I recognize them by:

(a)— how they move

(b)— the sound of their voice

(c)— what they look like

When daydreaming, I will catch myself:

(a)— fiddling with a small object

(b)— singing or talking

(c)— staring into space

Now add all the numbers next to the As, all the numbers next to the Bs, and those next to the Cs. Record them below.

(a)— = kinaesthetic

(b)— = auditory

(c)— = visual

Interpretation: the lowest number represents your strongest mode, the highest number indicates your weakest mode, the middle number points to your intermediate mode.

Chapter 1 summary
Sensory modes: How you learn

Sensory modes influence how you understand the world and relate to other people. The primary sensory channels are:

Kinaesthetic learner

- preferred format – note taking, recopying notes, outlining the book
- learns best with one other person (learning partner)
- information organization – the big picture, or overall plan

Visual learner

- preferred format – books, handouts, blackboard writing, notes
- learns best alone
- information organization – categorizing (mental spread-sheet)

Auditory learner

- preferred format – lecture, discussions with others, self-recitation
- learns best with a group
- information organization – relationships between facts

Special learning needs

- attention deficit disorder
- learning difficulties
- Most instructors are visual/auditory in nature and structure their teaching accordingly. Visual and auditory learners are served well in an academic setting.

- Applying the individual's sensory mode to the study setting that suits their needs results in more effective learning.

2
Your optimal study setting

Having found out what your personal learning method is, you should seek out an environment that nurtures it. One student's study distraction may facilitate another student's learning. Study guides typically suggest that you find a quiet, tidy, isolated area to study, such as the far corner of the library. While some students find this advice helpful, others may find it difficult to study in such circumstances. What is a distraction for one student may be essential to another for effective concentration.

Everyone has an optimal level of arousal. If the amount of stimulation (noise, movement, clutter) is above or below a certain level, then concentration may be hindered. Drinking coffee, for example, causes many people to concentrate better. However, after one cup too many, it's actually harder to concentrate.

To identify your optimal study location, assess a variety of areas for noise (auditory), clutter (visual) and movement (kinaesthetic). For some students, extreme quiet (deep in the library stacks) can make concentration impossible, whereas others find quiet allows them to stay on track more successfully. For some, a moderate amount of background activity and controlled commotion (common room, coffee shop) is optimal. For others, it is disruptive. Evaluate several different potential study areas and decide where you work best.

Heed the warning signs of overstimulation (inability to stay on task) and understimulation (nodding off or daydreaming) and adjust your learning locale accordingly. If you are a kinaesthetic learner, it may be difficult to stay in one place too long. Identify two or three different areas so that when you tire of one spot, you have somewhere else to go. Regardless of your memory style, studying in your own room may be risky because of built-in distractions such as phone calls, drop-in visits, food, television, the Internet, video games.

A word of caution regarding eyestrain. Remember your mother's warning to turn on more light when you read, for the sake of your eyesight? Her advice was right, but for the wrong reason. Low light actually saps your energy and ability to concentrate. Although you may be able to read in low light, your eyes have to work harder, causing you to run out of energy more quickly.

Your equipment

Most professionals prepare for a job by gathering the proper equipment. A surgeon collects her instruments before surgery. A salesman gets his paperwork ready before a sales call. And a teacher sorts through her notes and gets her overheads together before the lesson. As a 'professional memorizer', you need to surround yourself with the appropriate tools – dictionary, pencil, highlighter, watch, notepad etc. Since studying is distinctly different from your usual routines, you need to clearly signal your brain that the time has come to shift gears. Just as your mouth responds to the smell of a favourite food by salivating, your brain will respond to your study tools by starting to concentrate, which in turn can ease your mind into the proper framework.

Your personal distractions

Both physical and mental exertion tap into a common pool of body energy. When you are in a physical-need state, your mental efficiency will suffer. Being hungry, thirsty or tired can hinder concentration and learning. Don't ignore these physical needs and try to 'power' through the study material. You will remain inefficient and waste your time. Similarly, do not eat a big meal before studying. The extra blood needed in your stomach to digest food will not be available for your brain, so attention, concentration and memorizing will take more effort.

Two types of mental distraction can turn into study demons by pulling your attention away from learning – worry and unfinished tasks. Personal problems such as conflict with a friend, financial difficulties or family stress can consume considerable mental energy and gnaw at your concentration. All this makes you less mentally efficient. Another mental parasite is unfinished tasks – the cheque you need to post, the paper due, the phone call you have put off. Your mind gets stuck on these unfinished tasks, leaving fewer mental resources for studying.

To minimize a distraction, put a spotlight on it. Bring it into the open by writing it down. If the topic pops back to mind while studying, write it down again. Make a distraction log – whenever your mind wanders, record the time and content of your thoughts on paper or tape. Bringing mental ruminations under direct scrutiny lessens their impact.

Your energy cycle

Most people have a natural energy cycle during the day with a high (alert) and low (drowsy) period. Track your own cycle for several days, making note of the hours when you feel especially good and the time of day when you are drowsy. Then adjust your study times to maximize efficiency. During your drowsy period, do busy work – laundry, returning phone calls, shopping, cleaning your room. Study during your high-energy period. If possible, plan your timetable to coincide with your peak-energy stretches during the day.

Your motivation

It is a rare student who looks forward to studying. You may enjoy certain subjects or teachers, but it is hard to whitewash the drudgery of digesting, memorizing and revising material for an examination, even for the topics you like. To make this less painful, use small rewards to keep on track. Strenuous physical work requires occasional rest periods. Similarly, you need a break after hard mental effort. Change pace after each chapter, or hour, of studying. Study for an hour before a favourite TV programme. Study with a friend, breaking periodically to discuss the material. Don't make your rewards so pleasurable that they distract you from your homework or make it difficult to return to the task. Your motivation can also be enhanced by selecting teachers you enjoy or taking a course with a friend.

Planning backwards

The term often creeps up on you, bringing an avalanche of exams before you are ready for them. Plan backwards at the start of the term to avoid this trap. Create an assignment calendar, one month at a time. Mark all assignment due dates in one colour and then work backwards from these due dates and mark a 'start date' in a different colour. This will signal the beginning of a project in plenty of time to complete it. For each examination, mark the date a week ahead to begin your review, so that a test will never sneak up on you. Don't depend on your teachers or fellow students to keep you on track. The teacher may not remind you until the lesson before the test, and fellow students may assume that you are aware of it.

Chapter 2 summary
Your optimal study setting

Everyone has an optimum level of arousal

- seek out the environment that nurtures your method of learning
- assess area for noise, clutter, movement

Recognize when it's time to take a break

- overstimulation
- cycstrain

Elements of the proper study environment

- your equipment
- identification of personal distractions
- your energy cycle
- your motivation
- planning backwards

3
Basic truths about managing classroom learning

The typical pupil beginning secondary school has already logged more than 5,000 classroom hours. By the time pupils take their A-levels they have accumulated more than twice that. After so much experience, your classroom skills should be honed to a fine edge. Unfortunately, the typical classroom experience may lead to bad mental habits. It is a setting often made up of teachers who are boring or inefficient communicators, uncomfortable seats, hot rooms, social self-consciousness and inconsiderate fellow students.

The main barriers to managing the classroom experience are wandering attention and ineffective note taking. A passive attitude to learning leads to these problems. Some students liken their memory to a 'sponge' – if you pour the information on your brain, most of it will be absorbed. This passive model is not the manner in which your mind actually works. To memorize effectively, your brain must interact with the material. You must prepare your mind before the lesson and actively participate in the classroom experience.

Go to lessons – they are the easiest time to get a good grade

At the risk of stating the obvious, you should attend every lesson or lecture. Even if you don't like the teacher, attendance is optional, it is a bad time of day, you have a quiz for which you're already studying, or you are feeling exhausted – there is still no substitute for going to class. It is the only sure way to get the correct information and keep on top of the course. One of the most straightforward arguments for going to every class is to be sure that you are not caught unprepared for a test because you missed the reminder.

The second argument for going to lectures is to get the best set of notes – your own! Have you experienced an unusual event with friends and been surprised that your memory of it differs from theirs? This also applies to the classroom experience. Your memory of the details of the lecture cannot be replaced by someone else's written record.

While most students do borrow notes when they miss a lesson or lecture, many assume that they can get all that they missed by copying a fellow student's notes. But even copying the notes of a top student will not duplicate the experience of going to a lesson. When you attend, you remember details of the lecture such as asides, stories, discussion and blackboard material not in the notes, but in your mind, only to be recalled later. Absorbing new information is assisted by such contextual details – the sight, sound and feel of the situation where you learned it. Such 'contextual memory clues' become automatic access gates to the new memory. If you must borrow notes, then get them from two different students. This helps ensure that you don't miss any details and can identify important points by the overlap in the two sets.

Prepare your mind for the lesson

Review your notes

Before the lesson begins, cast your eye over your notes from the previous one. This prepares your brain for the new information – like ploughing soil before planting seeds. Refresh your mind on the topic so that less effort is needed to absorb new material. This quick review of class notes will also 'flag' areas that are confusing or incomplete. On occasion, a point that was clear at the time seems cryptic later. It's almost as if someone else had written the information in your notebook. A quick check helps identify problem areas so that the teacher can clarify them while the topic is still fresh. Such an inquiry will also impress the teacher, suggesting that you are keeping up with the material.

Read the set chapters

Thorough preparation for a lesson also involves reading the set material. Not only will it encourage a reasonable reading pace, it may generate other questions that you can bring up before the lesson. Pay special attention to words or phrases that are not clearly defined in the book. Have you ever bought a new pair of shoes and then noticed how others have started wearing the same type of shoe as yours? In reality, the world has not changed, but your attention has been sensitized. Similarly, the more your brain is oriented to the classroom material, the more readily the information will be absorbed.

Buy your books early, and begin reading before the first day of term. This allows you to get the flavour of the subject, get an idea of what to expect, and gain a headstart. Prereading will also help you identify courses that are not what you expected so that you can withdraw early without penalty.

Go to class early

Besides securing your favourite seat, getting to class five or ten minutes early will allow your brain to make an effective transition. Get out your pen and notebook, look over the previous lesson's notes, see what is written on the board and prepare your mind for what will be presented that day. Remember the last time you rushed into the lecture room late? After catching your breath and settling in, it seemed as if the remainder of the period was spent just catching up. By arriving late, you begin out of sync and risk missing valuable points as you catch up.

Appreciate the information-rich moments

All class periods are not created equal. The ones just before a test are often of special importance as the instructor may use this period to give tips on what to study (and not study) or what will be given special emphasis. If the teacher does not volunteer this, take the initiative to ask what will be covered, how the book or lecture will be weighted, how long the test is, etc. Another reason this pre-test class session is more important is that teachers occasionally fall behind in their lectures and have to compress several to cover all the material that will be in the test. Therefore, the last lecture before the exam is often richer in test material.

There are also information-rich times within each class period. General administrative comments are often made at the start of class – changes in test dates, cancelled classes, announcements about readings on reserve in the library. Students who come in late miss this information. If you come late, check with your fellow students. Don't depend on them to volunteer such information. The end of class is also important because the teacher may summarize the day's lecture. So don't shut down your brain too early – some gems may be dispensed at closing time.

Listen more effectively

In the classroom, the most critical skill is listening effectively. Most of us are lazy listeners since people are inefficient communicators. Typical conversation is filled with idle chitchat, and we get lulled into not paying close attention to what is said. Increased participation will enhance your listening abilities in the classroom.

Sitting at the front of the class helps effective listening by reducing distractions and intensifying the experience. In the first or second row, you are less likely to be distracted by activities both in and out of the classroom, and you will hear and see better. A big-screen TV is more engaging than a small one. A film at the cinema is more compelling than a video at home. Sitting at the front can intensify your involvement in the learning experience.

Participate

A good way to keep your attention focused is to ask questions during class. If you are uncomfortable raising your hand, jot questions in your notebook and ask the teacher afterwards. Listen with scepticism, noting inconsistencies between the book and lecture. Reflect on statements that generate possible examination questions. Don't struggle trying to mentally clarify a confusing statement because you will miss what is said afterwards. Read the teacher's body language to get a better appreciation of what is important and what is not. If they become excited, it is important. If they write it on the board, it is important. If they meander off on a personal story, it is probably unimportant.

Fight the mental fog

When your mind wanders to other matters, such as daydreaming about an imminent date or project, jot down the distraction in your notebook to get it off your mind. If you regularly drift off during a particular class, bring some coffee. Aside from contributing to alertness, research has shown that a small amount of caffeine can actually enhance memory formation. Yawning is a sign that your body and brain need more oxygen, so take a few deep breaths to correct this. Breathe in through the nose and out through the mouth. A small bit of physical stimulation can boost your alertness. So stretch your legs, wiggle your hands or shoulders, change position in your seat, etc.

Sharpen your note-taking skills

Use a double-sheet technique

Revising or condensing notes before a test is more difficult if you have to wade through extraneous thoughts in order to extract key lecture material. A spiral notebook, laid flat, has two sheets of paper to write on – one on the right and one on the left. Use the right side for the material presented in the lecture and on the blackboard. Begin each new class period on a new page with the date at the top, as it's easy to find later. Use the left side for additional comments or questions, points that need clarification, changes in due dates, details you need to look up, possible test questions, random thoughts and ruminations. Limit them to that page.

Leave plenty of space

When taking notes, leave blank lines between points. Don't be too compact. The cheapest part of your educational expenses is paper, so don't skimp. An instructor will occasionally get two things reversed, state something incorrectly or imprecisely, or simply leave out a particular point. With sufficient space, you can fill in missing topics or add corrections without making your notebook look cramped, cluttered and unreadable. Extra notebook space also allows you to add material later from a fellow student's notes or your own reflections.

Develop a shorthand

While the main ingredients of classroom learning are common sense, there are also 'tricks' that can be employed to increase the volume and accuracy of your notes. Because

31

we write more slowly than we talk, develop shorthand symbols to keep pace. A set of three or four standard abbreviations can make a big difference.

The following page contains a chart of suggested shorthand codes for taking quick and concise notes.

Shorthand code suggestions

about = a/b, abt
amount = amt
and = +, &
at, about, around = @
average = avg
background = bg
because = bc, b/c, bks, cuz, bcse
before = b/4, b/f
between = b/t, b/w, b/wn, btwn
change = Δ
continued = cont
definition = def
difference = diff
ditto = "
down (decrease) = dec, dn
each = ea
especially = esp
example = ex, eg
explanation = expl
for = 4
government = gvt
if and only if = fof
important = imp
in other words = aka
increase = inc
information = info
large = lg

leads to = →
left = ←
never = nvr
number = no
observed = obs
page = pg
point = pt
point of view = pov
produce, product = prod
reaction = rxn
regarding = re
relationship = r'ship, rel
right = rt, →
significant = sign
small = sm
somebody = sb
someone = so
sometimes, something = s/t
therefore = ∴
to, too = 2
up = ↑
with = w/
within = w/i, w/in
without = w/o
wrong = ←

- When a name is repeated often, use initials rather than the full name.
  WS = William Shakespeare
  TSE = T.S. Eliot
- If the name is very familiar or frequently repeated, you could simplify further by using the initial of the last name.
  F = Freud, *E* = Energy
- Truncate the word. The first three letters of many words substitute for the whole word, especially if you can get

the meaning back from the context of the notes or the word is used frequently in lecture.

rev = reverse
col = college
tec = technique

- Delete the vowels, and use only the consonants:

vwls = vowels
glty = guilty
prvd = provide

Slow down the teacher

A way to accommodate to the discrepancy between the teacher's speaking rate and your note-taking speed is to ask the teacher to slow down or pause for a moment. Ironically, teachers often speak faster when excited about a topic. It's especially important to slow them down when that is the case.

Tape-record your lectures

For auditory persons, taping lectures can be a great study aid. Most of you should consider this a supplement to, rather than a substitute for, note taking. Very few students can learn successfully by simply playing a tape recording. It can be a relatively inefficient technique timewise as it requires sitting through the entire lecture again. Take into consideration the extra time requirement. Always ask before you tape-record a lecture out of respect for the speaker.

Look over your notes immediately after the lecture

Your most effective revision is what you do just after the original experience because forgetting occurs most rapidly immediately after learning. Reading through your notes within an hour of taking them will accomplish more memorization than at any other revision to boost memory.

This immediate revision is beneficial in two other respects. If you inadvertently missed jotting down a piece of important information, the lecture will be fresh enough to recapture the missing point. In addition, material that appears to be clear in class occasionally does not make sense when you reread it. Mark these points for the instructor to clarify at the next lesson. If it makes no sense an hour later, it will certainly confuse you when you begin serious studying.

Coping with boring teachers

To be honest, some classroom problems can be traced to boring teachers who give monotonous lectures, ramble off on tangents, or repeat themselves. In fact, students overwhelmingly claim that boring teachers are the main reason for drifting off during class. While this is certainly a severe challenge to one's attention span, the situation is not hopeless.

Stay focused on these teachers by keeping track of repetitions. Tally how many times they clear their throat, say, 'you know' or 'OK', pull their earlobe etc. All teachers have these little quirks, and you have probably already mentally catalogued such habits many times before. You might think that this will take attention away from what the teacher is saying, but it focuses your attention on the teacher and makes you less likely to let your attention wander.

Your teacher as learning partner

View your teacher as a facilitator rather than an adversary. Many students assume an implied contest between themselves and the teacher. The teacher sets up learning hurdles to ensure that only the strong will survive, and you must work out how to manoeuvre around and through these obstacles to emerge with a good grade. The scorecard in this contest is the grade register.

Actually, most teachers derive satisfaction when students succeed and feel concerned when they struggle. Use your teacher as a resource. Ask questions, go to see them after class, tell them when something is confusing. Also keep in mind that teachers are human, and their opinion of you can influence your academic success. To keep their opinion of you intact, avoid the following:

- *Coming to class late* – It suggests that this particular class is not important. If you happen to arrive late, apologize to the teacher. This courtesy will be appreciated.
- *Shutting down early* – Several minutes before the end of class, some students close their notebooks, put things away and look at their watch. This suggests a mechanical student who is 'putting in time'.
- *Distracting behaviour* – Tangential activities during class, such as scanning a newspaper, reading a book, writing a letter, reading mail, talking and passing notes are usually noted by the teacher. It conveys the impression that you do not consider the class very important.

These methods set the stage for more productive learning. Now you're ready to develop a personal strategy for studying. In the next chapter, incorporate the information on sensory modes to accommodate your individual learning style.

Chapter 3 summary
Basic truths about managing classroom learning

Simple habits will improve your grade

- review notes prior to class
- read the set chapters
- go to class early
- sit at the front
- look over your notes immediately after the lesson

Taking notes

- use the 'double-sheet' technique
- develop a shorthand
- leave plenty of space

Class involvement

- participate in discussions
- go to every lesson
- sit at the front

4
Effective reading

Reading, for all its apparent simplicity, is one of the most complicated activities your brain performs. You must identify every letter you see and string the letters together to make a word. Then you must retrieve the meaning of each word stored in memory and connect all of them to make a coherent sentence. Numerous mental computations are made each second as you read. This process consumes considerable mental energy, so reading can make you drowsy even when you don't feel tired. This problem can be circumvented by easing into the material and coaxing your brain to keep on track.

Warm up your brain

Before physical exercise, you warm up your body. Prior to jogging, you stretch your muscles and tendons. Similarly, limber up your mind before reading. When you plunge into dense reading matter and find yourself reading the first page over and over, your brain has 'seized up' from being suddenly confronted with a demanding task.

Before you begin serious reading, read something light for five or ten minutes – a personal letter, a chapter in a pulp novel, an article in the newspaper, or your junk mail. This prepares your mind to handle the complex mental calisthenics involved in reading. If you have more than one type of academic reading to do, do the easier (more interesting) material first to help establish your rhythm. The more mentally limber you are, the better you will be at tackling dense information.

Reread the set matter

Most students read the text only once before the exam. Many students consider that sufficient. However, if you have the time it is better to read the assignment several times using the following method of layering.

Tackling the reading

Preview

First, survey the chapter for pointers on what is important – the preview paragraph, chapter contents and summary. Such information will provide clues about what the author considers important as well as a skeleton structure to guide your comprehension. Take special note of section headings, key words in bold print, pictures, charts, graphs, and date lines. Such textual embellishments usually emphasize key points.

Skim like a novel

The second stage involves a rapid read-through without concern for full comprehension. Don't worry whether a particular passage makes complete sense. Read it quickly as you would a magazine article or light novel. Most books have some dense passages wherein the author's point is unclear, but is instead clarified by the material that follows. If you find yourself bogged down in the middle of a confusing section, you may get frustrated and end up underlining everything in a desperate attempt to extract meaning. Worse yet, you may develop a negative attitude toward the book or course. Executing an initial speed reading, without a pencil, underliner, or excessively critical eye, can avoid this pitfall.

Digest for meaning

For the third pass, do an in-depth reading using a highlighter. Accent the central points. This will be relatively easy since you have already cleared a mental path via your early skimming. The preparation provided by stages one and two is similar to studying a road map before you drive somewhere new. The prior reading makes it much easier to keep on track and appreciate where the author is heading.

Review

As with looking at your notes just after a lecture, the most effective review of the textual information comes right after the initial reading, not the night before the exam. After reading a section or chapter, reflect on what you have just learned. What was the author's point? . . . key terms? . . . theoretical issues? This will not only solidify the information, but provide a quick check on comprehension – did you miss the main point or forget what was said just before? Put the material in your own words to make it more personal and memorable. Write your own summary of the text in a reading-comment notebook or in the book margins.

Once you've mastered this basic outline for effective reading, supplement the method with the following suggestions.

When preparing for the exam, go back over your underlining and extract the key terms and concepts. Use a different writing implement, such as a red pen, to accentuate key points within your highlighting. Create an outline of the reading. If you have time, continue to condense your reading notes into progressively more succinct outlines. Each pass at redigesting the material makes it more memorable.

Look up the word

Keep a dictionary at hand when reading. If you skip over words you do not know or assume that you will get the word's meaning from the context of the passage, you will lose the point of what you have just read. You will also waste less time by looking it up rather than guessing.

Mark up your book

If you bought your textbook, mark it up. Make it personal. Don't save a few pounds' worth of resale value to deprive yourself of the memorial benefit of personalizing the book. Marking your book aids memory in two ways. It increases your personal involvement with the reading, so you relate to it more deeply and remember better. In addition, the visual distinctiveness of your book pages is enhanced. Students often remember where something is on a page. They find themselves surprisingly able almost to see that term on the bottom right-hand side of the page with the orange picture of Europe at the top. This is not 'photographic memory', but a normal, visual image of the page. You have probably found over years of experience that certain book pages stand out in your memory – the ones that have unusual pictures, graphs or illustrations on them. If you customize your textbook with your own graphics and highlighting, you can create your own distinctive pages.

Jot notes to yourself in the book margin

Use different coloured pens. Fold the corner of important pages. Mark what you don't understand in addition to what is important. Develop a system of marking passages in a hierarchy of importance. For example, use a tick for moderately important points, a bracket around more important topics, and an asterisk beside essential points.

Read aloud

At primary school, you were told to avoid moving your lips when reading, or reading aloud, because it is inefficient and harmful to comprehension. Unfortunately, this restriction may hamper both the auditory and kinaesthetic learning channels. Give yourself permission to read aloud when you are alone, especially if you are an auditory learner. Although it is slower than silent reading, oral reading may improve comprehension and memory. Auditory individuals often do not complete their learning until the material is heard.

Fight the reading fog

All of us occasionally drift off when reading. This is especially likely when you jump straight into a reading assignment without warming up, the material gets dense, or you have been reading for a long stretch. Such mental wanderings often force you to read the same passage several times or to underline too much of the passage. Underlining everything on the page is usually due to being too tired to discriminate important from unimportant information. If you find yourself rereading or over-underlining, then take a break. Read something else for a while (a magazine article) or go for a short walk to clear your head.

If something mental is distracting you, write it down on a distraction notepad. The distractions lessen their hold on your concentration when brought out into the open. If you return to reading and are still not concentrating, try again later because you are wasting your time. If possible, don't read for more than 45 minutes to an hour without a break. Shorter periods interspersed with small rewards make the process less tedious and allow for more frequent reviews.

One final tip on effective reading – check the syllabus. It goes without saying that you need to read the right chapters for the test. However, a surprising number of students occasionally fail to check the syllabus to make absolutely sure that chapters they thought were on the test actually are. When taking five or six courses simultaneously, there is a chance that you could get the chapter numbers mixed up from course to course.

Chapter 4 summary
Effective reading

Prepare the mind for reading

- pay attention to 'reading fog' warning signs – rereading and over-underlining
- wandering attention means you're not learning
- warm up your brain on fun reading matter

Read with a plan

- preview, skim, digest, review
- look up unknown words before moving on

Check the syllabus

- confusion will waste study time

5
Digesting the information

By this point in your studying, you have already absorbed, written down, outlined, heard, copied and read the information you need for the forthcoming exam. Your next step is to digest, customize and personalize the information so that you can remember it efficiently during the test. Personalizing a new fact is like putting an identification number on a new book so that you can find it quickly and easily in the library stacks of your memory. The following techniques can help make these mental access routes more efficient.

Make it personal

Connect new information to personal experiences or what you already know. When a person describes his trip to Cancún, you'll remember better what they say if you have already been there. When someone discusses her dieting, you will better absorb her meaning if you also have dieted. If you can establish a link between new information and your personal experience or previously learned material, you will memorize more effectively.

Create flashcards

A time-honoured technique for learning mathematical formulae or a foreign language is flashcards, but they can also be helpful in learning any new terms and definitions. Keep a stack of three-by-five cards handy as you reread your text or review your class notes. Each time you encounter an important term, write it on one side with the definition on the reverse.

While many students use this technique, most do not use

flashcards effectively. Students tend to study in one direction – giving definitions from terms or reciting terms from definitions. If you practise recalling the definition given the term, but the test requires recalling the term given the definition, you may be stuck. Mental links between two things (word to word, word to definition) do not automatically work in both directions.

What letter follows 'T' in the alphabet? What letter comes after 'J'? Now, what letter comes before 'F' in the alphabet? What letter precedes 'Q'? You probably had more trouble answering the last two than the first two questions. Even though you know the alphabet 'cold', you always practise it in one direction – forwards. Reciting the alphabet backwards is difficult because memory links are weak through lack of practice. So you need to practise recalling the term from the definition as well as the definition from the term to be assured of success during the test.

To use flashcards effectively, go through the key words first until you can give each definition. Then turn the cards over and practise the other direction, giving each term from the definition. After you have practised in both directions, turn half of the cards over and shuffle the pack. This will allow you to practise recalling both directions at the same time (term to definition, definition to term) in order the better to duplicate the demands made during an actual test.

Set exam questions

Role-play the teacher and make up practice exam questions. It gets you thinking about the material in a way more suited to an examination. By identifying the terms, concepts and relationships that lend themselves to test questions, you view the material in the way your teacher does. Some topics easily lend themselves to test questions while others don't. Another benefit of creating and answering your own questions is that it provides practice for test-taking behaviour, being presented with a question and providing an answer. Writing your own test questions may yield an unexpected bonus – some items that actually appear on the test.

Repackage the information

When you have to remember a large set of terms or concepts – British prime ministers of the twentieth century or a hazardous-waste chemicals list – you benefit by using a specialized-list memorizing technique. While a variety of procedures are suited to this, the most popular technique (among students) uses acronyms, where the first letters of a list of words are converted into a term. For example, the five Great Lakes (Huron, Ontario, Michigan, Erie, Superior) can be condensed into the word 'HOMES'. The musical notes in the spaces of the treble scale are 'FACE'. The order of colours in the visual spectrum (red, orange, yellow, green, blue, indigo, violet) is summarized by the name 'ROY G. BIV'. Acronyms provide a compact retrieval path to regenerate an entire list of words or information.

Another process to help make remembering more efficient is grouping similar information together. For example, to memorize the US presidents you might group them into ones completing one term, completing two terms, and assassinated in office, or cluster them by political party.

Classic mnemonic techniques

There are three memorizing techniques that are the mainstay of memory-improvement books and seminars. While these techniques provide impressive results, they may be difficult to apply to academic material and become rusty without practice. These techniques are most helpful for a certain type of student who must memorize long lists of facts – such as medical students. Auditory and kinaesthetic individuals, who depend heavily upon visual imagery, may find them less user friendly. Bearing this in mind, I will look briefly at each procedure.

Chain and link

With this procedure, you form bonds between successive items in a list by a series of pair linkages or associations. The first item is connected with the second by constructing an interactive mental snapshot. Then the second item is associated with the third, the third with the fourth, using a similar image-construction procedure.

Suppose you have five items you need to buy at the shop – bread, cheese, tomatoes, milk and napkins. Your first image would involve the bread and cheese combined in some way, like a huge piece of Swiss cheese with a long, thin loaf of French bread stuck into one of the holes. For the second image, create a mental picture of a big kettle of tomato soup with large chunks of gooey cheese floating on the top and running down the outside of the kettle. In the third image, a large, ripe tomato is jammed into the spout of a gallon jug of milk, turning the entire container an odd pink colour. Finally, imagine a large puddle of milk spilled on the floor with an entire package of napkins used to mop up the mess. Armed with this package of visual images, you can work your way through the list at the store. Since each item in the list is part of two different images, each of the mental snapshots provides a clue to trigger another image.

Without looking back at the last paragraph, try to go through the list in your mind. Recall the first image and then allow this to remind you of the second image and so on.

Pegword

The pegword technique has the advantage of identifying the ordinal position of each item, such as item three on your list. With the chain-and-link method, you have to recall each successive image to locate the third item. However, the pegword technique allows you to identify quickly which item is third without searching through the others. You must first set up a master list of pegwords upon which to 'hang' each image. The typical one is 1-bun, 2-shoe, 3-tree, 4-door, 5-hive, etc. Associated with each number is a word that rhymes with it and that is used in making an associative image. Using the shopping list from the previous section, the first image is a bread sandwich – a loaf of French bread placed between two large slices of whole wheat. The second list item is cheese, and this could be imagined melted over a shoe. The third list item, tomatoes, could be seen as growing large on a big tree with many tomatoes fallen off and squished on the ground beneath the tree. For item four, a jug of milk could be visualized spilled all over the front door, thrown by a careless milk-delivery person. Finally, the fifth image is a beehive made out of napkins with bees buzzing away from the hive wearing tiny napkins tied around their neck.

As with the previous technique, stop for a moment and go through the pegword list (1 = bun, 2 = shoe, 3 = tree, 4 = door, 5 = hive) to see if the list word pops back into mind with each peg.

Location

The last list-learning technique involves using your memory of familiar living quarters with each room serving as a separate memory compartment. Each item on your shopping list can be pictured occupying a separate room or area, and a mental walk through the locations is used later to pull each item back to mind. Assume that a walk through your home will take you through the following five rooms – hall, living room, kitchen, dining room, study. First, imagine the entrance hall to your home piled high with loaves of bread, some of which are open and spilling bread slices over the floor. Next, you enter the living room, which has a large wheel of cheese as a coffee table with several mice nibbling around the edges. The next stop in your mental walk is the kitchen, where there are bushels of ripe tomatoes sitting on the counter ready to be cooked. Then, gliding into the dining room, you encounter one large pitcher of milk on the table, with glasses of chocolate milk at each place setting. Finally, you proceed to the den where you find napkins glued all over the wall in a quick attempt to wallpaper the room.

For each of these classic techniques – *chain and link, pegword* and *location* – you must make an extra effort to form the images. But once created, they are distinct and memorable. Make each image distinctive or exaggerated to enhance its memorability – crumble the bread, melt the cheese, tear the napkins, spill the milk and squash the tomatoes. If ordinal position is important – knowing which item is second or fifth in the series – the pegword technique is best. The location method has the advantage of a ready-made set of memory hooks, lessening the effort of making images.

Learn to music

An additional technique is available to music lovers. If you have a piece of music without words that you know well and can hum in your head, use it as a framework for remembering new information. One student familiar with a piece of music by Vivaldi used the music to format the course material. While studying, he would repeatedly read the outline against the background of a particular song, matching the rhythm of his recital to the flow of the music. During the test, he could hum the tune in his head to cue the information. You could form your information into a rap song and mentally sing the answers to yourself during the exam.

Spending part of your time studying with other students can play a role in effective memory. Find a study partner because some of the best learning can occur through modelling. Seek out the successful students in your class and sit next to them, taking note of what they write down. Find out how these particular students approach the material or which procedures they use to study. If parts of the lecture are unclear, check with one of these students afterwards.

Before you begin revising for the exam, check your notes against other students' notes. Discuss discrepancies, and add missing information to your set of notes. This provides extra revision, deepens your understanding of the material and may improve your note-taking skills by example. Also, compare your textbook highlightings, underlinings and annotations with a fellow student. Share your practice test questions with one another.

Participate in a study group

When faced with a large amount of material to digest and integrate, such as when you are coming up to your final exams, a study group may be beneficial. Several different explanations of the information establish additional memory-access routes. Explaining the material to others in the group deepens your own knowledge and helps you find the gaps in your understanding. As any instructor will confirm, teaching is the best way to learn. Don't split up the material and depend on someone else to digest a chapter for you. Read all the material yourself, and use others' summaries as a supplement.

In short, studying with fellow students can perform several special functions. You revise both by hearing points from them and by explaining issues in response. If you have arranged some revision sessions with a study partner, it will help limit your tendency to procrastinate. Although it is best to form an alliance with a more successful student, it is also helpful to collaborate with someone of equal ability.

Improve your revision strategy

Once information is successfully stored in memory, studying is not over. Successful recall depends on an effective retrieval plan. To find a library book, you need directions in order to get to it. Otherwise, it is of no use. Similarly, you must practise retrieving your stored information to make sure you can get at it later. Simply put, the access paths to your memories need, occasionally, to be rehearsed.

A common misconception about memory is that you can pound a fact into your brain if you rehearse it enough times. This rote, or passive, rehearsal is illustrated by the child staying after class to write, 'I will not talk out loud' on the blackboard 20 times. This mindless repetition is intended to etch the critical information in memory so that the pupil will not repeat the problem behaviour. Similarly, most students think that passively rehashing their notes several times before the exam will enhance their memory. But these simple rote rehearsals may not be strengthening the memory.

Active revision

Each time you go over the material, pay attention to it. If you are visual, close your eyes and make a mental image of your notes or create a mental picture of the information in an elaborated form. If you are auditory, repeat the facts aloud, explain it to a classmate, or discuss the concepts with yourself. Record yourself reading the information and then play it back while eating or driving. If you are kinaesthetic, several strategies are available to you. You can write down the information over and over again, copy the notes in condensed form, or create an outline of the book.

A couple of my students' methods have proved successful to them. One tries to fit all his notes on a single three-by-five card, forcing him to digest the class notes in a distinctive fashion and focus on the most important points. Another pretends that she is going to cheat in a test and condenses the key information onto a small 'cheat sheet'. This forces her to grapple with the information in an active manner and makes studying more engaging. These strategies work because they're individualized to the needs of the person.

Lengthen the revision intervals

The most important revision is when you have just heard the lecture or read a chapter. Memory research shows that forgetting occurs most rapidly over the first hour or so and then at a much slower rate thereafter. Revise new information soon after learning and then spread out the remaining revision – three hours later, that night, the next day, and then two or three days later. This revision plan provides the most retentive memory activity.

Study in small blocks

Be aware of your energy level as you are studying. If you find your mind wandering, stop immediately and write down your distracting thoughts to help deflate them. Your brain will not absorb the information if your thoughts are elsewhere. To avoid this problem, build in study breaks at regular intervals to prevent mental exhaustion. In general, try to study for no more than an hour at a stretch.

Learn from the test

Use the test results to improve your study strategy. Scrutinize the teacher's preferred format (types of question) and content selection (theory or terms, people or dates, etc.), as well as your own errors in studying for, and taking, the test. If you do not understand why you got an answer wrong, ask for clarification. If the instructor goes over the exam too quickly, call at his or her office later to look over the test more thoroughly.

Chapter 5 summary
Digesting the information

Use the information to its greatest benefit

- compose exam questions
- create flashcards
- new information

Classic mnemonic techniques

- chain and link
- pegword
- location

Study strategies

- participate in a study group
- use active revision
- find a study partner

6
Preparing for the test

Sitting an exam is like giving a performance. You practise recalling the information so that you can perform well under pressure or distraction in a way that is similar to a music recital, dance performance or play. It is not enough to have the information available under normal, comfortable conditions. You must be able to demonstrate your knowledge under duress. Furthermore, you must understand the conditions under which you are to perform (type of material, number of items, question format) so that rehearsal conditions create questions similar to that which exist during the test. Finally, you need to protect yourself from the harmful effects of stress and anxiety in test performance.

Find out what type of test to expect

It is quite distressing to walk into an exam and discover that the test format is drastically different from the one you expected. You thought the test would be multiple choice, but it is an essay instead. You were not expecting questions on the peripheral readings, but there are two essay questions on these articles. To avoid this minor trauma, do the following:

Ask the lecturer

Find out from the teacher what to expect in the exam – the format (short essay, terms, dates), length (how many pages), importance of each section, etc. Is there a penalty for guessing? Do poor grammar and spelling count against you? You have a right to know how your knowledge will be assessed.

Ask former students

Ask students who have already done a course with your teacher what the testing procedure is like. Even if it is a different course, teachers are creatures of habit. The testing format and grading policy will probably be similar. While teachers may be unable to assess whether their tests are hard or easy, former students can. Are there any quirks in how the teacher grades? Does the teacher appreciate extra information in essays? This knowledge can aid your mental preparation, help fine-tune your study habits, make your test performance more efficient and reduce your exam anxiety.

Use context to boost test recall

The conditions under which you memorize can influence the case of later recall. Whenever you learn something, you experience it in a context – a specific place (bedroom, library, classroom), wearing certain clothing (blue jeans, dressing gown), with (or without) other people and in a particular mental state (bored, sad, excited). Recalling information is easier when the conditions during learning are close to those that exist during recall.

Dressing in a formal dress or dinner jacket can trigger memories of a party long ago. The taste of strawberry ice cream may immediately transport you to a birthday picnic when you were 11. Memories often snap into place when the present context matches the context that existed during the original experience. When you learn academic material, the conditions under which you learn may influence how easily the material is recalled later.

In short, when studying, try to make your mental and physical conditions similar to those that will exist during the test. Does the following study scenario sound familiar? You slip into a dressing gown at 10.30 at night, get a cup of coffee and a packet of biscuits, and then lie on the bed with the radio or TV on in the background. People occasionally walk in and interrupt you. The phone rings, and you talk for a while and then idly trim your fingernails as you reread the textbook. This particular study setting is obviously very different from the conditions under which you will take the test. With a little effort, you can alter your study environment to resemble 'performance conditions' better and make it a dress rehearsal for the test performance.

Your mental state can be manipulated to your benefit. Research on 'state dependent memory' suggests that if you learn something in a particular mental condition, performance is best when information is recalled within that same mental state. If ordinary stimulants like caffeine or nicotine are used while studying, they should be taken again before (or during) the test. If you have three cups of coffee while studying, have several cups before the test. If you smoke half a packet of cigarettes during your study session, get some nicotine in your system before the test.

As with your mental state, the physical conditions under which you study can influence recall. Wear the same clothes you will wear during the test. Find a classroomlike chair to sit in while memorizing. Use the same pen, pencil and calculator during study that you will use during the test. Don't study in poor lighting conditions or with lots of people moving around. Turn off the TV and radio. To maximize these context effects, some students study in the same classroom where they will later sit the test. The day before the exam, find an hour or two when your classroom is empty, and spend time digesting and rehearsing the material while sitting there.

Practise writing answers

Most students practise recalling information by mentally running through lists or reciting aloud key points. This, however, is not the same technique you will use to demonstrate your knowledge. Since your test is written, practise writing answers. Actors do not rehearse their oral performance by writing or thinking their lines. Similarly, you shouldn't use oral or mental practice for a written test.

Allow plenty of time before the exam

A key difference between successful and unsuccessful students is effective time management. Even with exceptional mental equipment, time is the most precious resource in adequate test preparation. Most students (65 per cent) begin studying only two or three days before a test, and 84 per cent occasionally fail to finish the readings. Thus, the planning notebook discussed earlier is essential to scholastic success.

Two other study problems related to lack of planning are all-night revision sessions and cramming.

Most students occasionally stay up all night to revise when they have managed their time inefficiently. However, there are good reasons to avoid this. Fatigue can be devastating to your recall ability. In fact, one of the most common symptoms of physical fatigue is forgetfulness. Individuals who are 'worn out' are absent-minded, lose or misplace things, have trouble finding the right word, or forget important tasks. Thus, staying up all night can result in fatigue-induced forgetfulness during the exam. In fact, many students have horror stories about drowsing off or getting confused during an exam because of a lack of sleep.

Another problem with working through the night is that you are going against your normal mental cycle. Your mind is used to sleeping during the night hours, not absorbing new information. Thus, the effectiveness of three hours studying from 3 to 6 a.m. may be equivalent to one hour studying from 6 to 7 p.m.

Cramming is the second scourge of bad planning.

Cramming is an attempt to pound in the information at the last minute with a mental mallet. Some believe that they are packing new information into a temporary holding bin until they can 'dump' it on the test. However, this temporary memory only lasts for a few minutes at best. Cramming may also panic you as you face the inadequacies in your study plan or gaping holes in your knowledge. This emotional turmoil may further hamper your recall ability or block essential information. Finally, cramming can cause all the material to get mushed together. One of my students recently lamented, 'I had crammed to memorize a lot of formulas and molecular structures. But in the test, I got them confused and couldn't get the answers right.'

Protect yourself against exam nerves

Only the rare student feels no tension when taking a test. As noted earlier, stress can severely hamper your normal recall powers, shutting down mental operations and blocking your ability to get information out. While a little anxiety may help you get 'up' for the exam, too much can cause mental confusion and forgetfulness during the test. In fact, many students have experienced the nightmare of being so stressed out that they go totally blank during the test, to a point where they can't think of any answers. Although most recover, they remain shaken during the test and do not do as well as they should have. Here are a few suggestions to reduce or eliminate the negative effects of test anxiety.

Get your 'tools' together

Protect yourself against equipment failure during the test. It can disrupt your concentration if a pencil breaks and you have to borrow another or a calculator battery goes dead. Carry duplicates of all your tools to the test – pencil, pen, eraser, calculator. Avoid the wasted time and heightened stress that can result from lost, broken or malfunctioning equipment. Duplication is insurance against test panic.

Carry an emergency exam kit

Include aspirin and magnesium trisilicate for the occasional headache or stomach-ache during a test. Students often make strange noises during exams, so include earplugs in your emergency kit. Normally such sounds may not bother you, but when you need quiet for concentration and the students around you are chewing gum, talking to themselves, or cracking their knuckles, it may be a major distraction.

Come early

Arrive well before the start of the test. This allows you to get settled in, do some last-minute revision, find your familiar seat, and take several deep breaths to relax. Be careful about last-minute information exchanges with other students. Panic is contagious. If they are hyperventilating over the exam, you may pick up on this. Their information may be wrong, and this can easily confuse you. It is not the right time to get into a debate over the material. Even if they provide some facts that you somehow missed, you probably won't remember new information this close to the exam.

Learn relaxation exercises

A variety of techniques can reduce test anxiety – meditation, self-hypnosis and yoga. However, a simple relaxation procedure may suffice. If you feel overcome by stress during the exam, close your eyes, take in a deep breath through your nose, and let it out slowly through your mouth, blowing a continuous, controlled stream. Put your pen down for a moment, let your arms go limp at your sides, and imagine yourself in a pleasant, relaxing place. Practise controlled breathing and relaxing imagery before the test so you will be able to employ it quickly when the time comes. Knowing ahead of time that you can relax quickly lessens the likelihood that you will become anxious during the test.

Overlearn the material

Whenever professionals train for a performance, they overlearn what to do. Actors learn their lines for a part 'cold' a week ahead of opening night and then drill them in for the next six or seven rehearsals. Then, the stress of facing a live audience on opening night does not cause them to go blank.

You are also performing under stressful conditions during an exam, so you need to overlearn your information. Most students believe that it is sufficient to be able to repeat material from memory once to assure that they have learned it. However, many are surprised that during the test, the facts are not easily available. Think of extra rehearsals beyond 'one perfect recital' as assurance that the door to your memory will not shut owing to temporary distress.

Invest in your rituals

When confronted by anxiety, one way to ease its effects is to impose structure outside the test. This puts a measure of control and certainty on an otherwise vague and scary world. Many students engage in ritualistic behaviour to handle anxiety, and students often indulge in superstitious practices to cope with stress – what you wear to the test (specific sweatshirt, piece of jewellery, combing hair in a certain way), what you eat or drink in preparation (Mars bar, fruit juice, Polo mints), what you do beforehand (play loud music, pray, have a long shower). Don't minimize the importance of such habits. They can have a soothing effect prior to test performance.

Chapter 6 summary
Preparing for the test

Find out about the test

- ask the lecturer
- ask former students

Your mental and physical state

- practise writing answers
- study under the same conditions as the test

Protect yourself against exam nerves

- learn how to relax
- overlearn new material
- invest in rituals

7
Sitting the test

Now, for the test itself. You have only one chance to show what you know, and you need to prepare yourself for demonstrating your knowledge under adverse circumstances. The better prepared you are both mentally and physically, the better chance you have of demonstrating the full extent of your knowledge.

Ask the teacher

Students generally feel inhibited about asking questions during a test. Most assume that a confusing or vaguely worded question is an attempt to be subtle or tricky. It is very hard to write good test questions. They must be worded clearly, but in such a way that does not make the answer obvious. So ask if a question is unclear.

If keeping track of time is a problem, ask your teacher to remind you of the time remaining. Time management during the test is also assisted by knowing how many marks each question is worth. If not clearly indicated, ask the teacher how much each section (or item) is worth to allow you to allocate your time wisely. If time is limited, do the higher mark-value questions first.

Scan all items before starting

Just as you scan a textbook chapter before reading it, look over the entire test first. Don't attack the first question when handed the test, as if jumping off the starting block in a race. Instead, spend a minute skimming the entire test. Read directions twice. Students rushing through a test under time pressure often misread directions. Determine your pace by dividing the total time by the number of questions or the weighting of the items. This prevents the unwelcome surprise of finding a question worth many marks at the end of the test just as you are running out of time.

Some test information may not be as effectively memorized as it should be and be on the verge of being forgotten as the test begins. On your initial skim through the test, jot down any vanishing answer if you happen to hit upon such a question. You may also encounter questions about information that appears to have 'slipped away' from memory. If this happens, initiate a mental incubation process, similar to the one used to hatch an egg. Don't worry about the lost information. Put it out of your mind and move on to the next question. It may leap to mind while you are still sitting the test.

Teachers occasionally write several test questions related to the same facts or theories, and one question may contain clues to the answer of a related question. Skimming the entire test first may unearth this information as an aid to your recall.

Answer easy items first

After skimming, you are ready to attack the test. Instead of ploughing through all the questions in order, answer the easy questions first to build your confidence. Leave the more difficult ones for the second pass. There is nothing like boldly demonstrating your knowledge to boost your confidence on the other items. This also eases your mind into the question-answering mode, just like the warm-up reading that should precede dense textbook reading.

Mark up your test paper

Don't treat your test paper as fragile. Underline key phrases and words in each question to highlight the pertinent information and avoid distractions. Students are apt to miss an answer when they rush, misreading what information the question requires. Write notes in the margins as you go, develop the outline of an answer on the back of a page, eliminate multiple-choice alternatives by crossing them out. Indicate items you are unsure about with a question mark in the margin so that you remember to go back if time permits. Avoid making your paper messy, and keep your markings clearly outside the answer space. Always use a pencil and erase these markings before handing it in.

Write legibly and succinctly

One of the most tedious activities in the teaching profession is marking. Several hours of marking similar answers to the same questions is arduous, like hearing bad versions of a favourite song played over and over again. Under such conditions, a teacher may pay less attention to detail and look for the key terms, concepts and phrases. Even though you may be in a hurry, write as neatly as possible. Print if your handwriting is poor. Write larger if necessary. Underline the key terms in your answer – don't make the teacher hunt for them. It is especially frustrating to search through lines that are crossed out in order to decipher the correct answer scrawled in between the deleted lines. So if you tend to make mistakes or redo your answers, use a pencil.

With essay answers, keep it simple and to the point. If the teacher has waded through numerous similar answers, her patience and attention to detail may be running thin. Briefly outline your answer at the start, and then focus on the central information. But don't pad your answer to increase length (unless you have found out from former students that this is OK). This will only make the teacher work harder.

Managing objective test items

When confronted with any multiple choice, true-false, or matching item, first try to recall the correct answer before you make your selection. With multiple choice questions, cover the a-b-c-d alternatives as you read the question, and try to remember the answer on your own. After this, read all alternatives before choosing one. Don't just pick the first one that sounds correct.

When matching items, try to come up with the answer for the items in the A column without looking at what is listed in the B column. For instance, say column A has the names of scientific theories, and B has short definitions of the theories. You have to match the theory with the correct definition. Cover up the definitions without looking at them, and see if you can define the theory on your own.

Finally, don't go back over the test and excessively ponder whether you chose the right alternative. This may confuse you as rereading wrong answers makes them seem more plausible. It is better to settle for your first choice than to switch.

Managing memory blocks

Nearly every student has occasional memory blocks during exams. Although you can lessen the problem by overlearning and relaxation procedures, there will be times when you know the information, but it doesn't come to mind as needed. Don't try to squeeze it out. This will only increase your stress level, making it even less likely that the information will come to mind. Relax and close your eyes for about ten or 15 seconds. If it doesn't come back by then, move on. There is a good chance that the incubation process will work for you, with the stubborn information coming to mind on its own while you are working on a different part of the test.

If the incubation process does not work and you are still stuck when you return to the item, go through the alphabet letter by letter – say each letter silently, visualize it or write it down. Often, the answer will jump out at you when you hit on the first letter of the missing term. Also try thinking of peripheral information. If you cannot remember a name, try thinking of all the other information you know about the person. This will sometimes trigger the correct item by association.

Chapter 7 summary
Sitting the test

Sitting the test

- read the entire test first
- ask if a question is confusing; teachers don't always write clear questions
- pace yourself according to value of questions
- mark up the test
- write legibly for better understanding between you and the teacher

Managing memory blocks

- stay relaxed and wait only ten to 15 seconds before moving on
- the answers may come in a relaxed moment

8
The successful student

The survey used to gather data for this book was filled in by more than 400 sophomore, junior, and senior students at Southern Methodist University. This group of students was later divided into those with a grade point average (GPA) of 3.00 or higher and those with a GPA below 3.00. The responses of the higher group were compared with those of the lower group. While there was no difference between these two groups on many of the survey questions, there existed a statistically significant difference in certain categories that were key to study success. These are listed below. While sticking to these guidelines will not necessarily guarantee better grades, it gives a good profile of the study habits that engender success.

The better students:
- don't stay up all night to study
- don't 'cram' immediately before a test
- find their class notes clear when looking through them later
- don't study with background music or chatter (CD, tape, radio)
- don't study with the TV on
- are more likely to study by themselves than with a friend
- go over the material more often in their minds
- read set material for longer times at a stretch
- make up practice test questions
- don't go into a test unprepared
- rarely read or study the wrong chapters for a test

As a result of their study habits, better students:
- don't go completely blank during a test

- don't get anxious before a test
- don't get anxious during a test
- rarely suffer mental blocks during a test

So what can you learn from this description of the more successful student? They are better at time management and plan a sensible study schedule. This explains why they are less likely to cram, stay up all night or come to the test unprepared. This also leads to less anxiety before and during the test, as well as fewer instances of their mind going blank. More successful students also avoid the detrimental effects of study distractions (radio, TV, CD player) and are aware that the best use of their study time is alone. They also know the value of getting the teacher's perspective by making up practice questions. Finally, their proficient note-taking skills allow them to understand their own class notes clearly later on.

A final word

Your active participation in your own education is one of the most valuable decisions you'll ever make. The discipline and organization that accompanies the strategies introduced in this guide will improve not only your educational performance but also your performance in the world beyond the classroom. When the skills acquired at school carry us successfully beyond the classroom and into the world around us, we know that our education is complete.

I hope I've provided you with a new perspective on the art of studying. These principles will increase your chances of getting better grades. The satisfaction of earning grades that reflect your potential will make your school experience into one of achievement for which you can be proud. So give it your best try. Good luck!

Alan S. Brown

Overall summary

The information assembly line

- New information passes through three stages – sensory, working, long-term memory
- Pay closer attention – capturing the new information before it slips away
- Make effective associations – packaging new information for effective storage
- Active revision – lubricating the access lines to your memories

Your unique memory style

- Kinaesthetic learner – learns best from note taking, recopying notes, outlining the book
- Visual learner – learns best from books, handouts, blackboard writing, notes
- Auditory learner – learns best from lectures, discussions with others, self-recitation
- Special learning needs – attention deficit disorder, learning difficulties

Your study environment

- Establish your optimal study setting – avoid understimulation and overstimulation
- Equip yourself – get a dictionary, pencil, highlighter, clock, Walkman
- Recognize your physical distractions – hunger, thirst, fatigue can sidetrack you
- Deal with your psychological distractions – worry and incomplete tasks sap your mental energy

- Map your energy cycle (morning, afternoon, evening) – study in high-energy periods
- Motivate yourself – reward yourself after each study session
- Plan backwards from test date – make a start-date calendar for each term

Managing classroom learning

- Go to lessons – they are the best time to get a good grade
- Get your mind ready for the lesson – look over the last day's notes just before the lesson
- Pay attention to important class times – first five minutes of each class, last class before a test
- Improve your listening ability – sit at the front and ask questions about the lecture
- Sharpen note taking – use lots of space, develop a shorthand, review notes after the lesson
  * Drifting off in class – boring lectures and distractions will do it
  * Coping with mental drift – intensify your note taking, keep your eyes on the teacher
  * Managing your teacher – treat him or her as a learning facilitator, not a TV set

Effective reading

- Warm up your brain – do light reading to ease into the reading
- Go over the reading several times – preview, skim, digest and review
- Look up new words – don't assume you will work out their meaning
- Annotate your book – personalize with your own markings

- Read aloud – learn from your own voice
- Pace yourself – understand your reading rhythm
- Watch for the reading fog – rereading the same page, over-/underlining
- Check the syllabus – make sure you read the right chapters

Digesting the information

- Personalize new information – relate it to your own experience
- Make your own flashcards – put key terms on one side, definitions on the other
- Compose exam questions – get into the head of the teacher
- Repackage the information – use acronyms and grouping
- Use classical memorizing techniques – chain and link, pegword and location
- Learn to music – associate the information with the tune, then hum silently during the test
- Find a study partner – compare class notes, book underlinings, generated questions
- Participate in a study group – if you dare
- Learn from the test – know what style to expect the next time
- Improve your revision strategy – pay attention to what you are revising
- Establish your pace – plan backwards from the test, and cut it up into small bits

Revising for the test

- Know what type of test to expect – ask the teacher and former students
- Use context to boost later recall – make your study state match your test state

- Avoid cramming and staying up all night – this burns your brain
- Protect against exam nerves – learn relaxation exercises, overlearn the material

Sitting the test

- Your emergency exam kit – gather your test-taking tools and remedies
- Ask the teacher – if something is unclear, just ask
- Scan all the questions first – get your timing down
- Answer easy questions first – build your confidence
- Mark up your test – highlight key terms, outline your essays
- Write legibly and succinctly – print answers, use a pencil
- Manage objective tests – recall before peeking at options, stick with your first choice
- Manage memory blocks – stay relaxed, give it ten to 15 seconds and then move on

Bonus tips for success

Troubleshooting

PROBLEM	SOLUTION
Unfair tests	
Material on the test wasn't covered	Don't make assumptions – ask the teacher
Tests measure more than regurgitation	Expect to apply what you learn
Tricky questions	It may be a bad question rather than a tricky one
Tests from hell	
'My mind's gone blank'	Monitor your personal stress level, fatigue and level of preparation
Physical distress	Let your teacher know that you are ill before the test
Study gambling	If you skip a section, be prepared for the consequences
Fatigue	Bring some stimulation – even a sharp pin!
Exam room distractions	Bring earplugs, or ask to change your seat

Successful student profile

- Study without distractions – turn off the TV, radio and CD player
- Keep your cool – find ways to deal with nerves both before and during the test
- Take clear lesson notes – be sure that they always make sense to you later
- Study alone – your time is more efficiently spent on your own
- Manage your time well – don't cram or stay up all night
- Do practice questions – get into the mind of the teacher
- Do your advanced planning – double-check that you are reading the right chapters

Notes Section

NOTES SECTION

NOTES SECTION